My Dirty Little Secrets

A book of hope and love.

My Dirty Little Secrets

By Teresa Young Wesley

PaSH Publishing
Birmingham, Alabama

Published by PaSH Publishing

Copyright (c) 2017 by Teresa Young Wesley

All Rights Reserved

Published in the United States by PaSH Publishing, an imprint of The Southern PaSH Company.
www.SouthernPash.com

PaSH Publishing and its logo are owned by The Southern PaSH Company.

Book cover art by Fashionlistically Speaking
Layout done by Kaneshia Sims Hudson

ISBN
978-0-9992852-0-6

Printed in the United States of America

First Edition

" For God hath not given us the spirit of fear, but of power, and of love, and of a sound mind."

2 Timothy 1:7

My Dirty Little Secrets

Introduction

Understanding My Friends

Manic depressive disorder is a serious brain disorder in which a person experiences extreme variances in thinking, mood and behavior. Alcoholism is a chronic disease characterized by uncontrolled drinking and preoccupation with alcohol. My personal definition for manic depressive disorder and alcoholism are "My Dirty Little Secrets".

Millions of people suffer from mental illness everyday. They walk around attempting to function, not knowing they have a mental illness, I know this is true

10   My Dirty Little Secrets

because, I was one of those people.

Writing about my mental illness is healing for me. It is a therapy that I can't get any other way. My biggest wish is for my story to elevate God and bless someone in the process.

It is my opinion that we should live in a world that embraces people with mental illness. People born with a mental illness don't get to choose it. The mental illness chose them. Existing and never living is what my life is like seventy percent of the time. I have decided that existing is the beginning and I get to write my own ending.

About The Author

Teresa Young Wesley

Teresa Wesley is a member of Saint Bartley Primitive Baptist Church in Huntsville, Alabama. Teresa has worked as a nurse since 1984. Through her experience as a nurse, mother and follower of Jesus Christ, Teresa hopes to help people encounter God by uncovering and revealing their true selves. She hopes her journey will enable people to help others.

Teresa currently lives in Huntsville, Alabama with her husband Tim. Teresa has three daughters, one son in-law and two grandsons.

12   My Dirty Little Secrets

My Dirty Little Secrets

Chapter One

Growing Up Normal

I was born on January 16th, 1963. I was born in a small town by the name of Atmore. Until recently, the town was known for its prisons located near by. Now, the town is known for its popular casino.

I am the second born of five children. My mother had three boys and two girls. While growing up, I had friends and I was considered to be one of the popular kids. Although popular, I was shy, friendly and made good grades.

14   My Dirty Little Secrets

After high school I went to college. In college I studied hard so I could become a nurse. I worked as a nurse for a year before I married my high school sweetheart. Two years later, I started a family totaling three beautiful girls. That is when I woke up.

I don't confess to be anyone special or have any magic tricks that I could show you. What I do have are life lessons and experiences. I have a wish for this book to continue to help me grow and heal. I also have hopes that this book will be a healing tool for others as well.

In my African- American family, mental illness is not anything you discuss with ease or comfort. To many, mental illness appears to show weakness or punishment for past sins you have committed. When the word mental illness is used, people usually think of words like "cursed". Often, the word mental illness is used in sentences with words like rejection, shame and crazy. For

My Dirty Little Secrets

me, the words mental illness are my "Dirty Little Secrets".

Mental illness does not care if you are educated, rich, beautiful, male or female. It can be deceiving and strip you of your self-confidence.

Friends and family look at me and see a confident, intelligent, go-getter, who some may even say is attractive. These are words people say when you grow up normal.

There is nothing normal about manic depression disorder. The effect it has on your relationships, finances and employment can be damaging for everyone. I am here to confirm that there is light at the end of the tunnel. Manic depression is a condition, it is not a life sentence of doom. I have learned that you have to surround yourself with people who love you enough to know just as much, if not more, about the condition as you do.

16   My Dirty Little Secrets

Surround yourself with people who care enough to see you for who you are. Don't surround yourself with people who will label you and classify you as the mental illness, but look at you as a person who needs a lot of extra tender care.

Chapter Two

Misdiagnoses

For many years I had zero energy, drive, desire or anything that excited me. I was hurting in secret and trying to survive for my family. I had no desire to survive for myself. My family is the thing that kept me fighting and striving to live. I can't honestly pinpoint the time in my life when everything became clear to me regarding my mental disorder. What I can remember, vividly, is how I felt after I had my first child. That is when I noticed changes in my moods. There were periods of extreme sadness and feelings of worthlessness. Since I just had a baby, I wrote my feelings off as postpartum depression. Unfortunately, the symptoms of my diagnosis of postpartum depression continued until I gave birth to my second daughter, which was almost two years later. In other words, the feelings of sadness and worthlessness never went away.

Over the years, doctors gave me antidepressants that didn't work. Unfortunately, I continued to feel like the life I was living was not worth living. I never felt 100 percent myself no matter what I took or no matter what I did. To be honest, it was all so confusing to me.

During my adult life I was diagnosed with anemia. Anemia is a condition that causes a person to have low iron. The symptoms of anemia are feelings of being tired, having low energy and being irritable. Shortly after the anemia diagnosis, I was diagnosed with fibroid tumors in

My Dirty Little Secrets

my uterus. At that point, it started to all make sense. This had to be the reason I have had all the sadness, tiredness, mood swings and no desires to speak of! I finally had a diagnosis for all my troubles, so I thought.

Shortly after the diagnosis of fibroids and anemia, I was given iron transfusions and a high iron diet. After several rounds of treatment my condition did not improve. My doctor suggested a hysterectomy and I agreed. After my procedure, my iron levels were almost normal.

I was confused to why I still had feelings of doom. I would make excuses for my feelings by telling myself all I needed was a little more time to start feeling like my old self again. Almost a year had passed when the symptoms of despair intensified.

Up until that point, I had been able to hide what I

was going through, until it started to affect my job. The sadness, feelings of worthlessness and mood swings made it hard for me to go to work or get out of bed.

God has always blessed me with great paying jobs all in management positions. I was good at what I did and was often promoted for my hard work. I felt guilty for not being able to get out of bed and provide for my family.

As time went on, my mood swings and sadness increased and my desire to get out of bed, go to work and even live, decreased. Often, I left work early due to the overwhelming feelings of doom and worthlessness. I feared there was no way out for me. I was misdiagnosed for years.

Chapter Three

Covering the Facts

Secretly, I began to research my symptoms. My appointments with doctors and therapists were short lived and a waste of time. I was never fully honest with any of the medical professionals. I was ashamed to discuss everything that was really going on with me. Instead of being honest, I told them just enough to deceive them. During my visits I would reveal just enough to be diagnosed with conditions such as situational depression. Situational depression occurs when someone experiences death of a loved one, loss of job or something along those lines.

22   My Dirty Little Secrets

I figured that depression was depression and any medication would do. That was before I started my research and discovered that I was very sick and needed help.

After years of denial, I finally had to realize the truth, I had manic depressive disorder. It took me a while to adjust and accept the condition that chose me.

Many times I wanted to confess my mental illness to my husband, mother and even friends. I hesitated because I feared rejection and humiliation. At times I would start conversations about manic depression and it would be mocked in conversation. People would say jokes and use terms that made me sad. Jokes like, someone forgot to take their crazy pill or that person should be locked up. Statements such as those made me hide in shame. As I stated before, African Americans such as those in my family, do not put a lot of merit in mental health. If you speak of people having a mental illness, it is considered a

My Dirty Little Secrets

curse and never taken seriously, therefore, mental illness is never discussed or understood in many African American families.

As time went on, new symptoms were appearing and the old symptoms were magnifying. For years, I had sleepless nights, I would go without sleep for days, sometimes weeks. To help me sleep, I was prescribed sleeping pills that would not work. The pills would only allow me to sleep for a very short period of time. During my periods of insomnia, I would have lots of high-energy moods. During these "highs" I would start projects that I never finished and engage in activity that I never thought I could participate in otherwise. During my "highs" I felt like Superwoman!

24 My Dirty Little Secrets

During periods I call my "lows", I would become sad, tired and could not get out of bed. Bathing, dressing and combing my hair seemed like such a tremendous job. During the lows, my desire to do anything was such a challenge. I started calling myself names such as lazy, crazy and confused. I knew I should be doing everyday activities but I could not find the strength or will to do them.

During my journey, alcohol was my friend. Typically, I was a social drinker. Only drinking with friends or while out. But, after I discovered alcohol made me sleep for hours, I would drink heavily to fall a sleep at night. Drinking to fall a sleep had its consequences. As I drank more often to fall a sleep, my need to consume alcohol increased. Wine, my drink of choice, did not have the same affects. I had to turn to the hard stuff, vodka, rum, and whiskey.

My Dirty Little Secrets

As I continued to use alcohol to cure my insomnia, I discovered that drinking intensified my symptoms. I would become aggressive and verbally abusive. I would have periods of my life just disappear. I would find myself not remembering parts of my day or night.

Things were getting really bad and out of control. I found myself having trouble keeping a job for long periods of time. At one point, I had over ten jobs in an eleven month period. I know it is a normal thing to get up, go to work and take care of your family. But, for me, it was a struggle just to get out of bed. With everything inside me, I would attempt to get up and function like a normal person but the feelings of worthlessness, sadness and despair would always win the battle.

So finally, I decided it was time to discuss my illness with my husband. I needed help from someone I loved to help me figure it all out.

26   My Dirty Little Secrets

My dirty little secret was destroying my marriage and my relationship with my children. It was destroying my entire family.

After talking with my husband, spending hours explaining myself, confessing and revealing all my flaws through rivers of tears, my husband, at first, showed signs of concern. We both agreed to read the information regarding my condition. Unfortunately, it never happened.

I tried to explain to him that stress triggered my periods of "low". I tried to get him to understand that the less stress I encountered, the likely hood of my experiencing a low period would decrease.

One night, in an attempt to give him a visual aid, I rented a movie about mental illness. The movie was suppose to be informative, instead of learning, he only mocked me and said I needed to join the real world. For me, this is the real world!

My Dirty Little Secrets

That was the moment I realized I was on my own. Not even my husband would try to take the time to understand.

The hurt of rejection put me into an entire new ball game. My wedding vows stated in sickness and in health. This chain of events led to my wake up call. I was on my own and the best way to deal with it was to confess. I had to confess in a way that would be healing for me and prayerfully, others, who feel the world does not understand them.

28　My Dirty Little Secrets

Chapter Four

The Wake Up Call

Confessing to my husband about my mental condition was a big step for me. I thought we could get through anything because we were so in love. We were soul mates. I had to quickly and painfully get over the rejection and go on with my life. But first, I had to forgive my husband. I had to realize that there are situations in life that people just can not accept or deal with. So, after a lot of crying and a lot of praying, I forgave my husband and moved on with my life. That point in my life is what I refer to as my wake up call. It was exactly what

I needed. It put me in a position where I had to come out yelling and shouting, " I have a mental illness". The mental illness is not who I am. The illness does not define me! Anyone that has been afraid, anyone that has been ashamed, please do not be. Wake up, there is life in spite of your illness.

Please believe me when I say, there are people who understand and people who care. I need for you to confess, share and believe you are worth loving, you are worth living. Take your medication, continue your therapy and communicate with your loved ones. There is incredible life for all of us. Wake up and live life. Uncover your dirty little secrets. Realize that you are still deserving of all that life has to offer. All you need is a little love and tender care.

Chapter Five

Removing the Clown Face

One of my favorite verses can be found in the bible under Second Timothy, chapter one verse seven. It reads: " For God hath not given us the spirit of fear, but of power, and of love, and of a sound mind."

What a beautiful verse, it makes me feel whole and complete every time I read it.

I want to elaborate on "sound mind". God gave us the spirit of a sound mind. That spirit is what I have decided to tap into, hold onto and claim for the rest of my life. First, I had to remove the clown face.

The clown's face is a face we design and make up to deceive and survive. It is the face we walk around with in order to cover the shame and rejection we don't deserve. It is the face that covers the hurt and the guilt that we feel when we can't get out of bed using sheer will-power.

This is the time to remove the layers and come alive with who we really are and who we are striving to become. It is time to wash the corners of your mouth and remove the lipstick. Use your bare lips to speak of the spirit of sound mind that exists within all of us. Now is the time to remove the clown makeup from around your eyes. With uncovered eyes, allow the world to see that you have a soul and a life worth living. Remove the powder from your nose and smell the roses. Smell the victory that is before you. Remove your clown's face and make your claim as a person and not a condition. We are made

My Dirty Little Secrets

from the image of God and God is beautiful.

34 My Dirty Little Secrets

Chapter Six

Great Minds Think Alike

Struggles of any kind cause a person to reconsider decisions and choices that were made in life. No matter if the struggles consist of the loss of a loved one, financial problems, or getting over addiction. The mind can play a powerful part in how a person deals with mental illness. The mind can be a strong as well as a destructive tool when dealing with mental illness.

During my journey with mental illness, destruction was all I considered. As a born again Christian, I now know that my Lord and Saviour was crucified on the cross for our sins and rose on the third day. Now, all I feel is peace, joy and the will to live.

I am living proof that the life we live is based on how the mind is fueled and what we feed the mind to thrive on. Fuel your mind with the word of God, the way of God and the love of God. Life changes begin with your way of thinking and determine if you will be added to the list of great minds that think alike. Change your way of thinking and watch your life change. All great minds think alike.

To those who suffer with mental illness or have loved ones with mental illness, greater and better days will come by being informed and educated about your illness. It will allow you to focus on life and not your condition.

My Dirty Little Secrets

Chapter Seven

The Perfect Face

To anyone who is reading this book, you are not alone. There are so many of us in bondage and not just with mental illness. Surviving day to day is challenging, but we can do it. You have a perfect face underneath all the layers of makeup. Remove your clown face and reveal your face. Your face is original, one of a kind and unique, it is the perfect face. I bet if you remove your clown face others will think your face is perfect as well.

God Bless,

Teresa.

38   My Dirty Little Secrets

My Dirty Little Secrets

Dedication

To the Ones I Love

This book is wholeheartedly dedicated to my Lord and Saviour, Jesus Christ, and to my dad, Joe Young Sr, known to many as Wes. He has gone to soon, but he will never be forgotten.

Also to friends, family and ex-husbands who shared my journey.

40   My Dirty Little Secrets

My Dirty Little Secrets

Acknowledgments

Thank you

I would like to express my sincere appreciation to my daughters, Kaneshia Sims Hudson, Shaneice Sims and Keiontra Brooks, for loving me in spite of me. They were my reason to survive. I love them dearly. Mom, I want to say thank you for listening and being my prayer partner. You never stopped loving and guiding me. To my husband Tim, who supported me financially. My son in law, Warren Hudson, for supporting the entire family in our times of need. To my grandchildren, Jaylen and Giovonni, I love you both.

www.ingramcontent.com/pod-product-compliance
Lightning Source LLC
Chambersburg PA
CBHW050547300426
44113CB00012B/2302